5TH GRADE SCIENCE WORKBOOK: LIFE SCIENCES & BIOLOGY

Speedy Publishing LLC
40 E. Main St. #1156
Newark, DE 19711
www.speedypublishing.com

A series of activities that will review a Fifth Grader in the Following Life Science and Biology Lessons:

- ➲ THE HUMAN BODY

- ➲ GENETICS

THE HUMAN BODY

Show to every fifth grader how the human body is interconnected with these worksheets. They'll learn how the different organs and bodily systems function to keep us on the go.

THE HUMAN BRAIN

Label the parts of the human brain on the next page. Just pick the answers from the choices below.

Brain stem

Pituitary Gland

Thalamus

Hypothalamus

Medulla

Midbrain

Cerebrum

Ventricles

Cerebellum

Pons

Corpus callosum

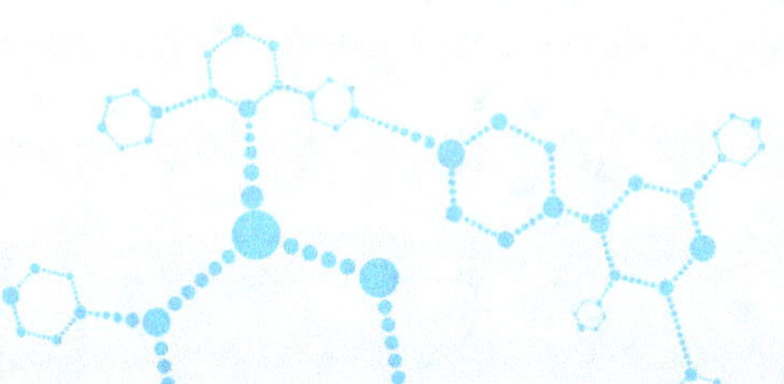

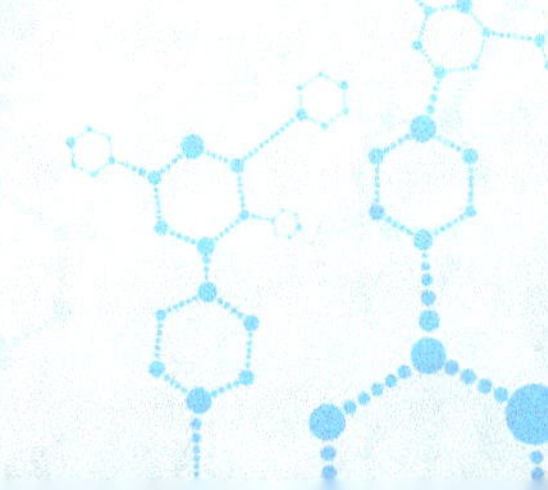

HUMAN BRAIN

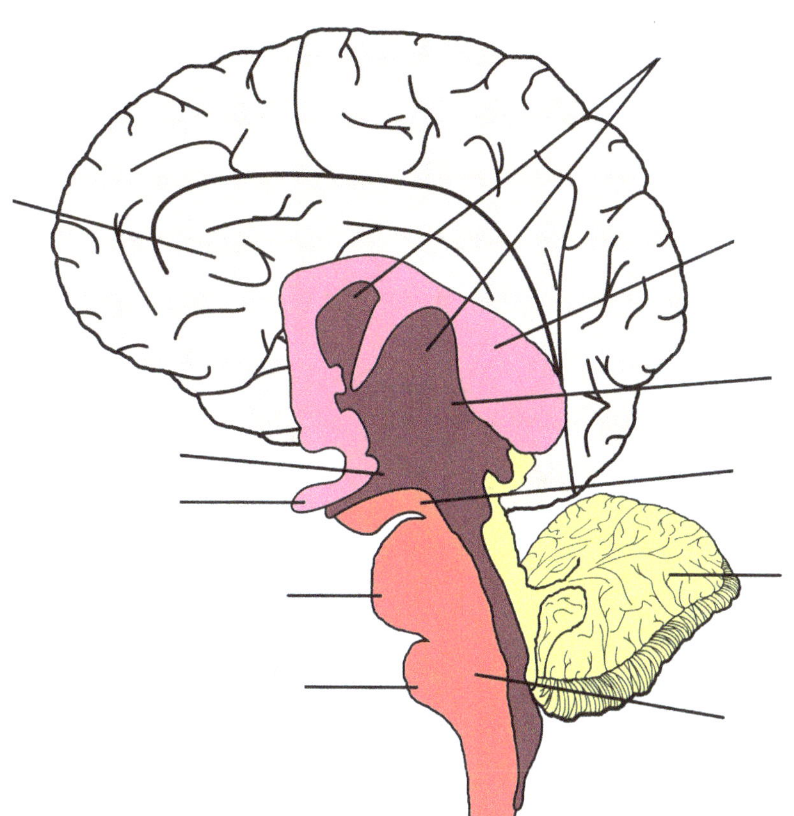

Identify the external parts of the human heart from the next page. Just write your answers on the blanks provided below.

1. _______________________________

2. _______________________________

3. _______________________________

4. _______________________________

5. _______________________________

6. _______________________________

7. _______________________________

External Anatomy of Human Heart

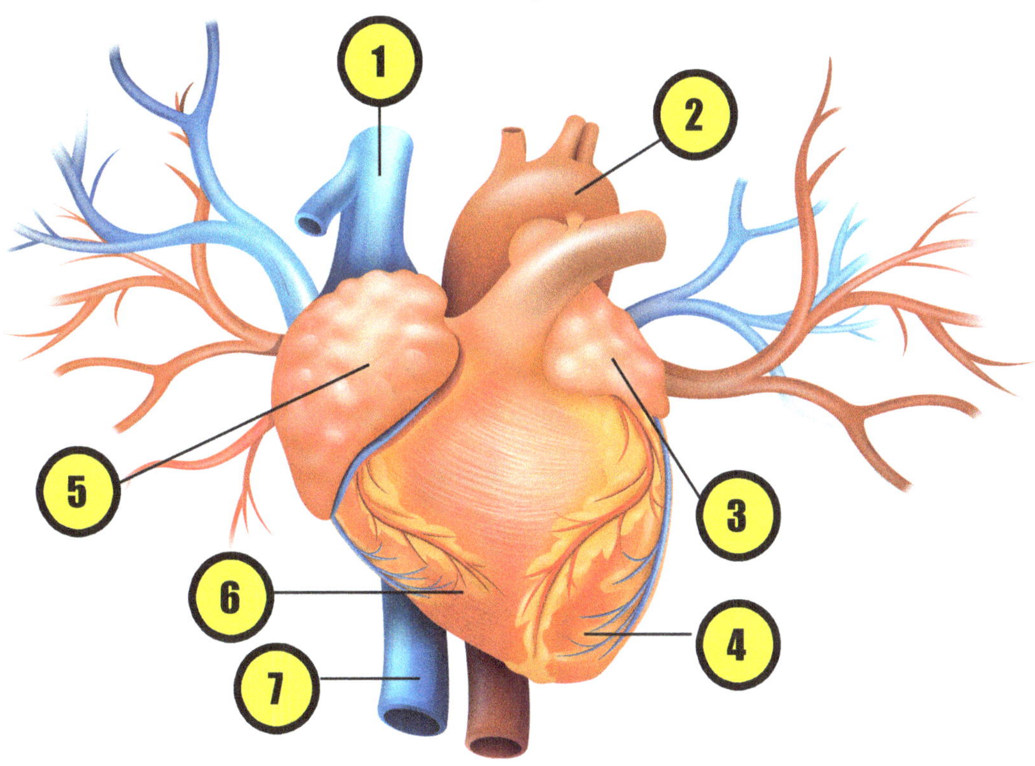

HUMAN LUNGS

Label the parts of the human lungs on the next page. Just pick the answers from the choices below.

Bronchi

Right middle lobe

Pleura

Larynx

Diaphragm

Trachea

Bronchial tree

bronchi

Right inferior lobe

left superior lobe

Right superior lobe

Left inferior lobe

HUMAN LUNGS

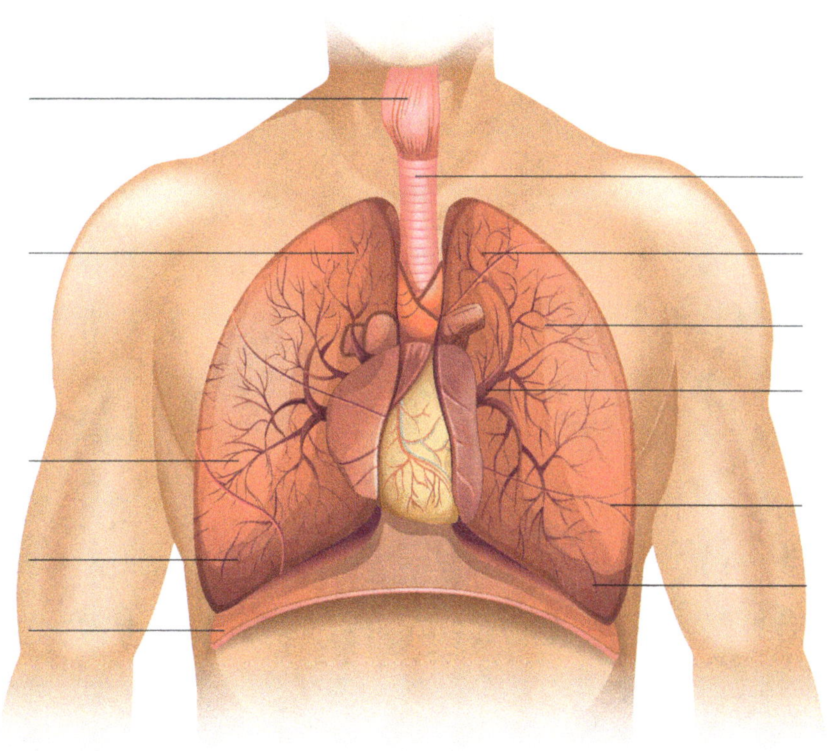

Identify the parts of the Digestive System from the next page. Just write your answers on the blanks provided below.

Anus	Sigmoid colon	Descending colon
Liver	Stomach	acending colon
Rectum	Ileum	Hepatic flexure
Esophagus	Cecum	Jejunum
Appendix	Cuodenum	Flexura of
Gall bladder	Pancreas	transverse colon

DIGESTIVE SYSTEM

Identify the parts of the human internal organs from the next page. Just write your answers on the blanks provided below.

1. _______________________
2. _______________________
3. _______________________
4. _______________________
5. _______________________
6. _______________________
7. _______________________
8. _______________________
9. _______________________
10. _______________________
11. _______________________
12. _______________________

HUMAN ORGANS

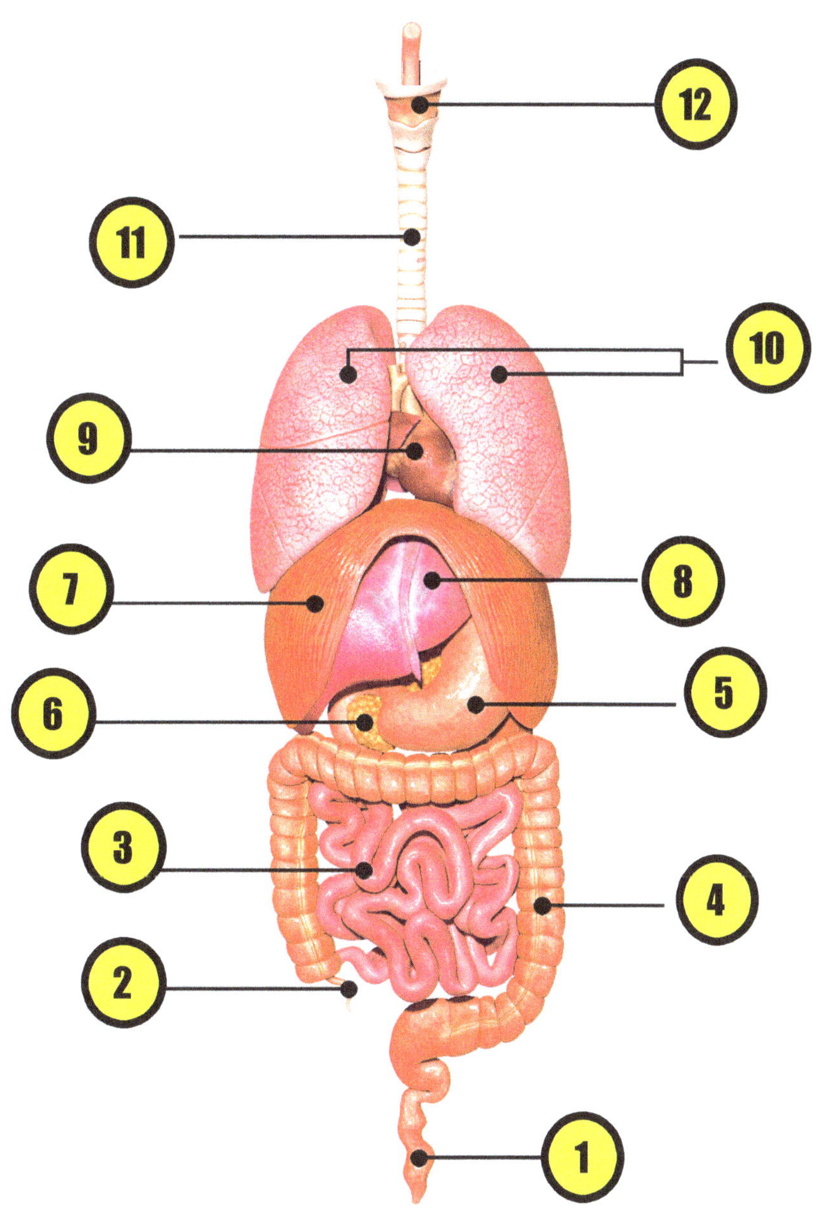

GENETICS

Series of activites to make a fifth grader
understand how genetics affects
every living thing in the world.

GENES, DNA and CHROMOSOMES
You draw 😊 if the statement is TRUE and 🙁 if the statement is FALSE.

_______1. You Have 22 pairs of Chromosomes.

_______2. A chromosome is made up of DNA

_______3. Everyone has genes.

_______4. Every persons DNA is unique.

_______5. We inherit Chromosomes from our parents

_______6. Genes determine what your body looks like.

_______7. Chromosomes are found in the nucleus of every cell

_______8. A blank DNA is called "Empty DNA.".

PLANT CELL

Draw and color the different parts of a plant cell beside the specified boxes based on the Plant cell image in the next page.

- Microtubules
- Cytoplasm
- Cell Membrane
- Nucleus
- Nucleulos
- Mitochondrion
- Golgi vesicles
- Golgi apparatus

PLANT CELL 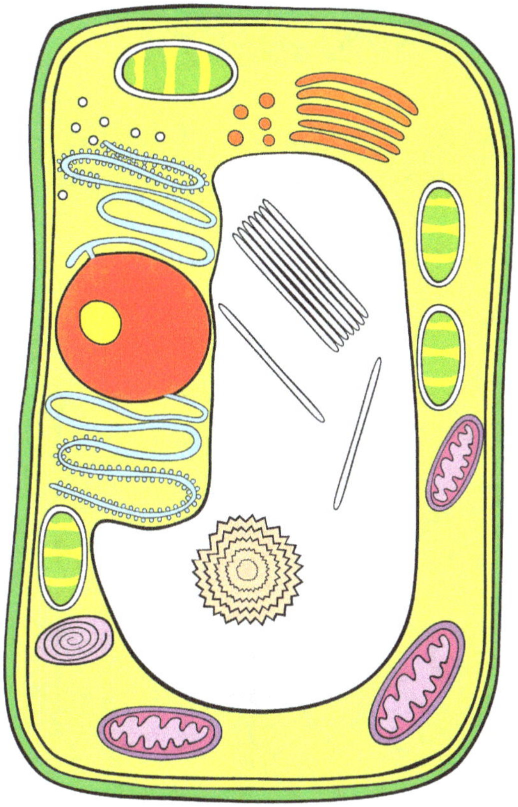
Cell Wall
Raphide Crystal
Endoplasmic Reticulum
Ribosome

ANIMAL CELL

Draw and color the different parts of an animal cell beside the specified boxes based on the animal cell image in the next page.

☐	Chloroplast	☐	Nucleulos
☐	Amyloplast	☐	Mitochondrion
☐	Cell Membrane	☐	Golgi vesicles
☐	Nucleus	☐	Golgi apparatus

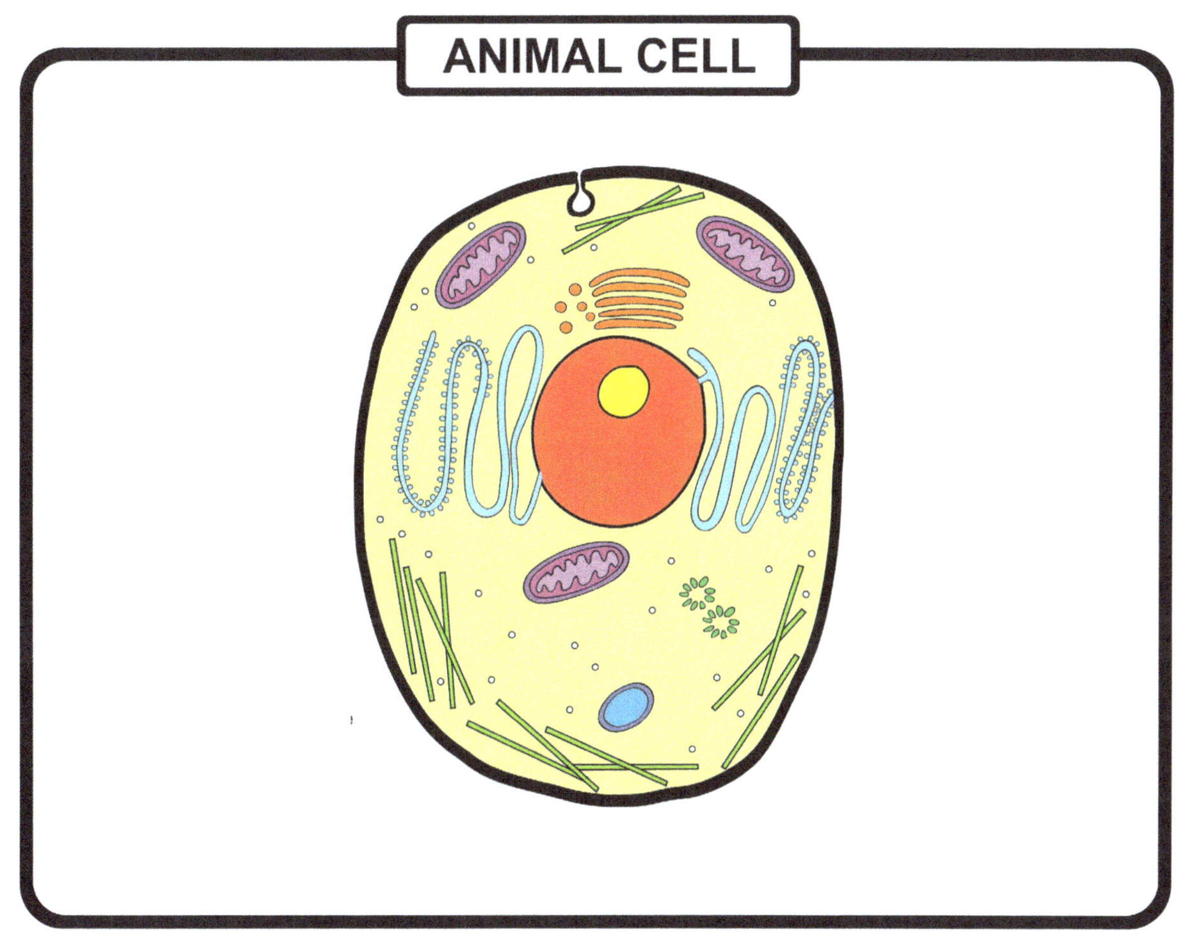

Centrioles

Ribosome

Lysosome

Pinocytotic
Vesicle

CELL DIVISIONS

Show to every fifth grader how a parent cell divides into two or more daughter cells

Label the chronological process of Mitosis in next page. The different phases are listed below.

Telophase

Prometaphase

Prophase

Anaphase

Cytokinesis

Metaphase

CELL DIVISION
(mitosis)

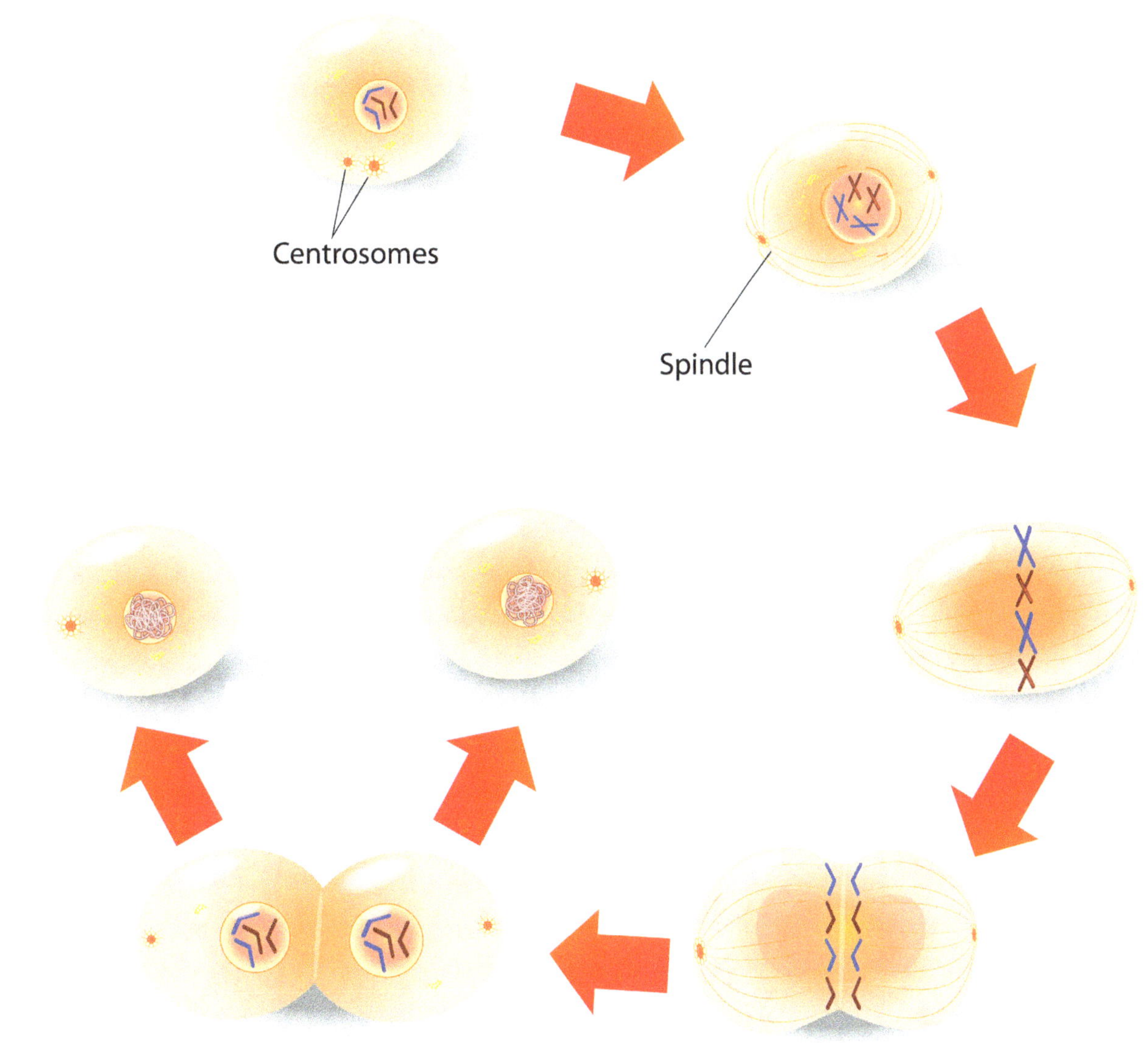

MEIOSIS

Label the chronological process of Meiosis in next page. The different phases are listed below.

Interhase

Prophase

Anaphase

Cytokinesis

Metaphase

Telophase

CELL DIVISION
(meiosis)

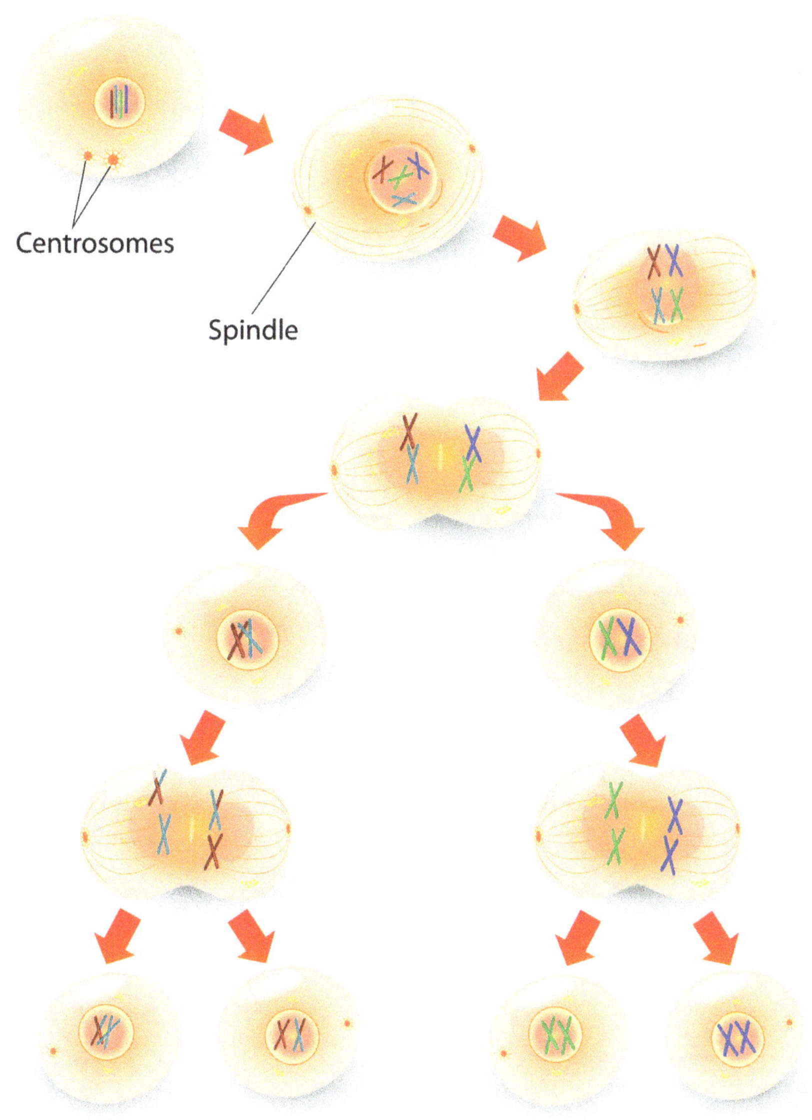

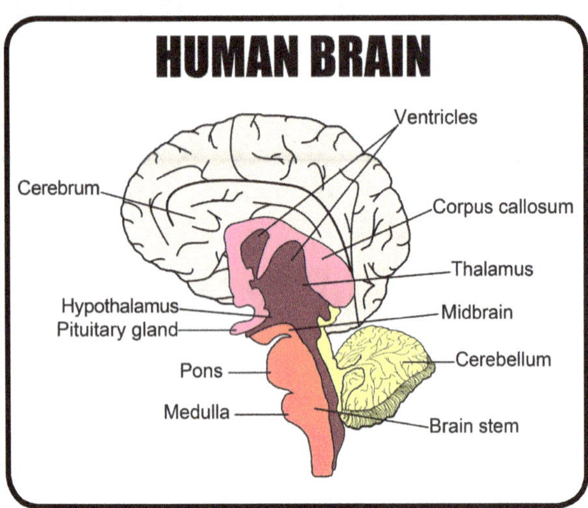

HUMAN BRAIN
Cerebrum
Ventricles
Corpus callosum
Thalamus
Hypothalamus
Pituitary gland
Midbrain
Pons
Cerebellum
Medulla
Brain stem

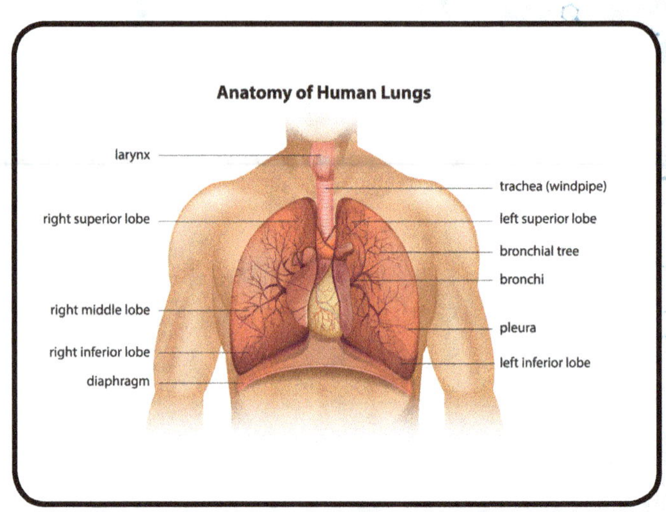

Anatomy of Human Lungs
larynx
trachea (windpipe)
right superior lobe
left superior lobe
bronchial tree
bronchi
right middle lobe
right inferior lobe
pleura
left inferior lobe
diaphragm

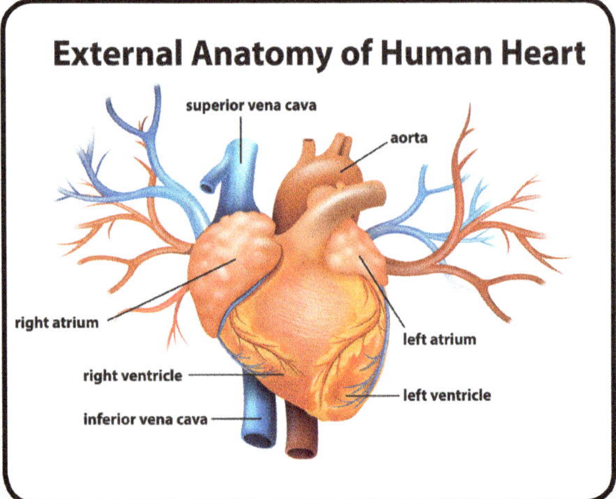

External Anatomy of Human Heart
superior vena cava
aorta
right atrium
left atrium
right ventricle
left ventricle
inferior vena cava

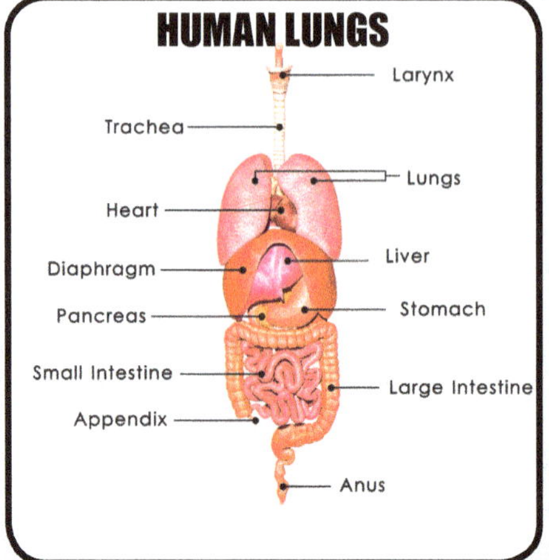

HUMAN LUNGS
Larynx
Trachea
Lungs
Heart
Liver
Diaphragm
Stomach
Pancreas
Small Intestine
Large Intestine
Appendix
Anus

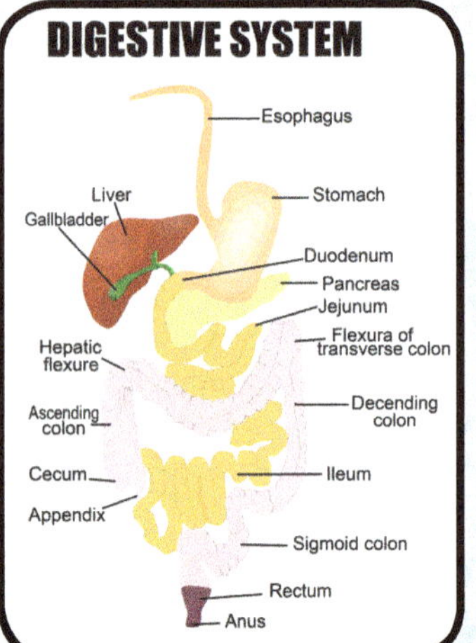

DIGESTIVE SYSTEM
Esophagus
Liver
Stomach
Gallbladder
Duodenum
Pancreas
Jejunum
Hepatic flexure
Flexura of transverse colon
Ascending colon
Decending colon
Cecum
Ileum
Appendix
Sigmoid colon
Rectum
Anus

GENES, DNA &
CHROMOSOMES
1.
2.
3.
4.
5.
6.
7.
8.

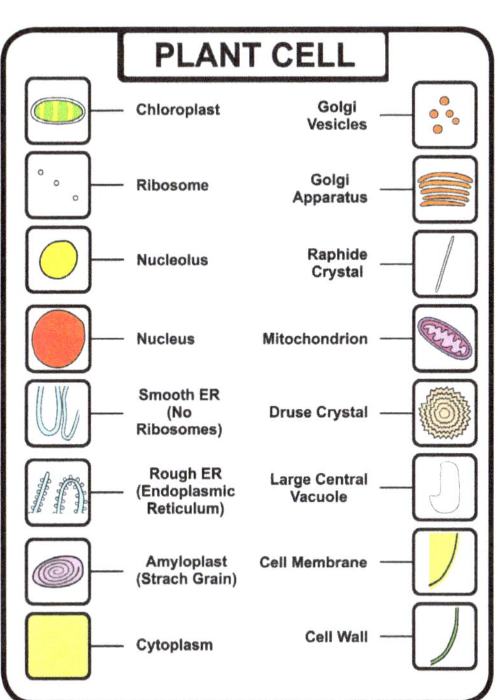

PLANT CELL
Chloroplast
Ribosome
Nucleolus
Nucleus
Smooth ER
(No Ribosomes)
Rough ER
(Endoplasmic Reticulum)
Amyloplast
(Strach Grain)
Cytoplasm
Golgi Vesicles
Golgi Apparatus
Raphide Crystal
Mitochondrion
Druse Crystal
Large Central Vacuole
Cell Membrane
Cell Wall

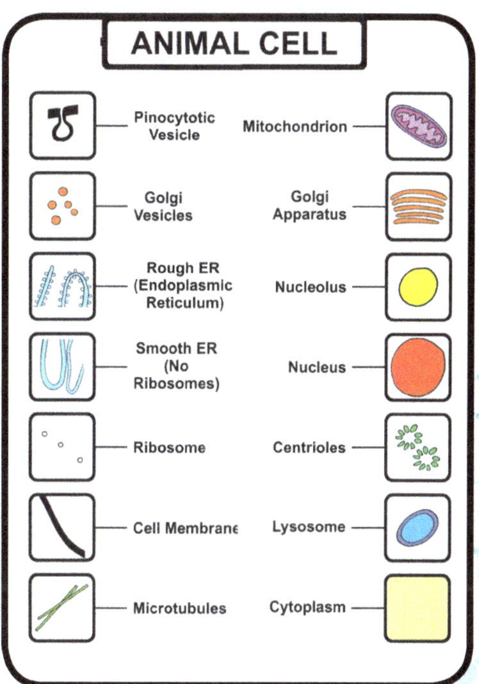

ANIMAL CELL
Pinocytotic Vesicle
Golgi Vesicles
Rough ER
(Endoplasmic Reticulum)
Smooth ER
(No Ribosomes)
Ribosome
Cell Membrane
Microtubules
Mitochondrion
Golgi Apparatus
Nucleolus
Nucleus
Centrioles
Lysosome
Cytoplasm

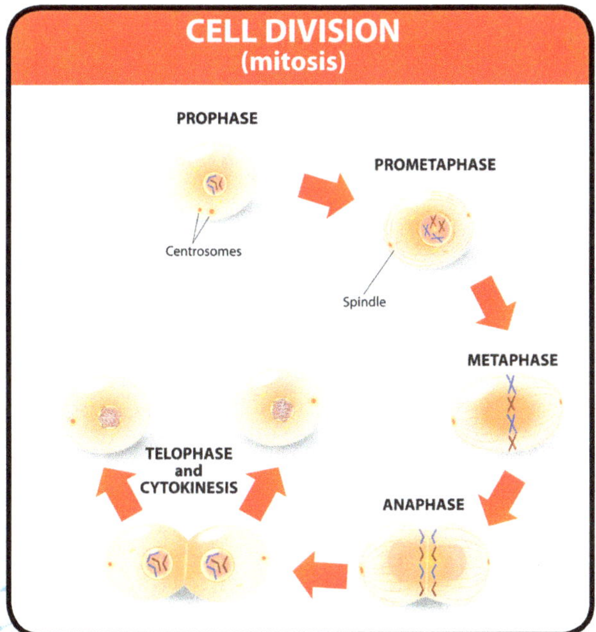

CELL DIVISION
(mitosis)
PROPHASE
Centrosomes
PROMETAPHASE
Spindle
METAPHASE
ANAPHASE
TELOPHASE
and
CYTOKINESIS

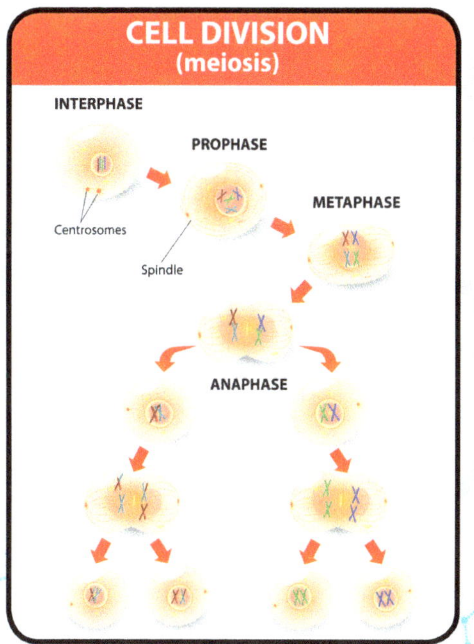

CELL DIVISION
(meiosis)
INTERPHASE
PROPHASE
Centrosomes
Spindle
METAPHASE
ANAPHASE